UNABLE FOR THE WORLD TO SLEEP

Poems by

Tom Ruud

L A U R E L
P O E T R Y
COLLECTIVE

ACKNOWLEDGMENTS

"January" previously appeared in *Sidewalks* (May 1992); "America" in *Mankato Poetry Review* (Summer 1993); "Hwy 61" in *Flyway* (Spring 1997); "Subtext" in *The Park Bugle* (November 1997); "Frodo in the Yard" in *Mankato Poetry Review* (as "Summer Letter," May 1997); "West of Grand Forks" in *Flyway* (Spring 1997); "August" in *Minnesota Monthly* (August 1998); "Caesura" in *Southern Poetry Review* (Winter 1998); "May" in *100 Words* (June 1998); "Garden Mary" in *Talking River Review* (Fall 1999); "North Shore Sublunar" in *ArtWord Quarterly* (Summer 1999); "Joan in the Wood" in *Water~Stone* (Fall 2001); "Snow God" in *A New Name for the Sun* (St. Paul: Laurel Poetry Collective, 2003); "It Was a Dark and Stormy Night" in *A View from the Loft* (June 2003); "Antiphonal" in *Pulling for Good News* (St. Paul: Laurel Poetry Collective, 2004); "Who Knew" in *Love Letters*, a chapbook anthology (Laurel Poetry Collective, 2005); and "I Knew All Along" in *Bluefire* (St. Paul: Laurel Poetry Collective, 2005). "sonnet nine one one oh one" was published as a letterpress broadside, Georgia Greeley, artist, by Laurel Poetry Collective, 2003.

Epigraph: Deborah Keenan, "Grace," from *The Only Window That Counts* (St. Paul: New Rivers Press, 1985).

Thank you to all Laurels, especially members of my small group: Ilze Mueller, Eileen O'Toole, Su Smallen, and Pam Wynn. To Margaret Hasse, Deborah Keenan, and Jim Moore, wonderful mentors who read versions of this manuscript. To students, especially my Monday Poets, who read some of the poems included here. To Hamline University faculty and staff, especially Margot Fortunato Galt, Patricia Kirkpatrick, and Mary Rockcastle.

© 2005 by Tom Ruud

All rights reserved.

ISBN 0-9761153-6-0

Printed in the United States of America.

Published by Laurel Poetry Collective
1168 Laurel Avenue, St. Paul MN 55104

www.laurelpoetry.com

Book design and graphics by Sylvia Ruud

Library of Congress Cataloging-in-Publication Data

Ruud, Tom.
    Unable for the World to Sleep : poems / by Tom Ruud.
       p. cm.
    ISBN 0-9761153-6-0
    I. Title.
PS3618.U93U53 2005
811'.6—dc22

                                                2005026606

*for Sylvia—
all the years,
every one*

CONTENTS

PART ONE: *you found me everywhere*

Snow God	11
Easter Lullaby	12
Early Episodes	13
It Was a Dark and Stormy Night	16
Dad's Squirrel	17
All Ones	18
First Death	19
Still Life with Sisyphus	20
Unbroken Chain	21
Aunt Inga's Abstract Print	22
Gethsemane Window	23
Hwy 61	24
Revision	25
I Knew All Along	26

PART TWO: *and holding them up to your eye*

North Shore Sublunar	28
Sundogs Rising	29
The Face You Almost See	30
West of Grand Forks	31
May	32
October	33
The Clearing	34
Sharpened	35
To Bravery, Late	36
Subtext	37
January	38
Antiphonal	39
Iphigeneia	40
Hound of Earth	41
America	42
August	43
Narrative	44
Frodo in the Yard	45
Last Year's Web	46

PART THREE: *leaning into something unseen*

Imago Patris	48
A Road	49
Dad's Lamps (Two Beauties)	50
All the Usual Cars	51
Appointment	52

The Home	53
Stroke	54
The Founding Fathers	55
First Marriage: Syntax	56
Who Knew	57
July	58
Eyesore	59
How We've Done It for—Years	60
November	61
My Life, So Far	62
Experience	64

PART FOUR: *Shall we go down?*

A Gnostic Gospel	66
All Hallows' Eve	67
Jeremiad	68
sonnet nine one one oh one	69
Before Pilate	70
Garden Mary	71
Joan in the Wood	72
Elvis	74
She Told Me the Story of Her Life	75
At Orchestra Hall	76
Aubade	77
Then	78
Caesura	79

PART ONE

you found me everywhere

Snow God

I am a fort made of snow,
perfectly temporary,
and the snowballs there
at my back wall,
they also will drip
over a warm curb
and into the caverns.
And those boys,
pounding up the steps
and in for soup, heads
about doorknob high,
will soon enough
lie in graves,
slowly coming apart,
the water running
away with them,
as water will.

Yes, and myself,
as I sink this spring
into my favorite yard,
I will think of your mittens,
so cute, making me,
and of the will you found
for rough beginnings, patting
pieces of protection together—
and you found me everywhere.

Easter Lullaby

Lie still now, lie still in your bed,
don't dwell on the terrible darkness.

Turn that way, to face the door,
and light in yourself a lantern
to see by. Thrust it up
over the monstrous heads

if you can, when they appear.
No parents, no brothers or sisters
now—you are alone, there
under your sheet, against them.

Those who take
your dark bedroom closet
as their crease, who snake
between the oldest clothes,
emerge from the backmost
forgotten boxes, clad in nothing
day-lit, who rise in slow shapes
and misshapes, eyes and arms
laden with onslaught—for them

roll the stone away, shine light
into their speechless cave.

Early Episodes

       i.
Lilies, perhaps, and leaves
repeating on wallpaper, prisoners
of pattern, they run to the ceiling,
down to the floor, stand stalled
in the corner, creased mid-body—
through crib bars, waking
to see it so, caught in this room.

      ii.
Simple sums, always wanting nouns
to count; four sisters, three brothers,
sixth child, third son, ten quiet plates
around the dining room table—my fork,
four tines, picking at too many peas.
"Sit there, then!" Forever?
Numbers run loose, grow
on their own into teens,
up into hundreds, orderly,
new through thousands, millions—
an immense immanence
yet to be minted in things,
while Plato waits, still sixteen
years away.

      iii.
Unusual hour, blackened glass
for the eclipse, neighbors
like a biblical flock spread
on the slope of Tower Hill,
all turned toward the sun
burning above the trees.
The blank coin of the moon

rolls over the world
of ordinary light;
mid-morning dusk snuffs
across the hill, sends the birds
back to bed; while I, daring
to go blind, watch the ring put on,
the fire we never see.

   iv.
An inch of summer air
between my heel and night hands;
the game of thresh and winnow,
of bringing the wild to bay, it comes
as a call from the crowded middle:
"Pom pom pullaway, come or else
we'll pull you away." With blood
of Mars, shadow of Venus, I can be
any part of the sky tonight, fly
my own planet in the yardlight.

   v.
Crackle of leaves, October grass
combed clean, piles smouldering,
barrels burning in open regret,
the haze that hangs
in empty trees: an incense
over winter—let it come.
So the rite is done,
and snow does come,
the same as memory,
to little mystics in snowsuits,
mute as angels, pressing out

the shape of flight
in a cold white drift.

                vi.
Stiff new shoes,
off to school, Fall,
pencil, paper, satchel,
past the tire swing
hanging dead straight from the elm,
off the ground, a zero
with rope aimed through the boughs,
past the treehouse, sky, and clouds—
into blue Heracleitean fire,
the climb off the planet beginning.

It Was a Dark and Stormy Night

Writing my first novel in a little spiral tablet,
big number two pencil, thunder, lightning,
invisible Titans shaking the bottle of my
made-up mansion, my murky road—I keep
erasing, writing over smudges, forever on
the first page, primping my shocked still life
like a painter in a shadowy studio.

It has to have that crazed incandescence,
that berserk tympani of thunder, a howling
wind, Beethoven's hair in the trees—it has to
match that night, not long ago, not far away,
exploded from a stifling day, the living room,
the bubble of childhood, bursting in the middle
of a world storm, house shaking, trees falling,
Dad in the yard like a sea captain, wrestling
the tumbling porch screens from the wind.

But it won't find that place on the couch
beside my mother's fleshy hip, her summer
nightgown cool, her arm curling me into
safety, the carnal center of fate. It cannot go
back to that, stuck though I am on page one.

Dad's Squirrel

It would come seeking him
in the yard, tail flicks
tethering out its fear, closer,
and then quick up his leg
and dig in his shirt pocket
for the seed, race across his back
and dive down to the ground.
Not amazed, I thought
the world would be like this,
the warm pocket, the seeds,
the happy dash back to the box elder.

All Ones

He came home one payday
with all ones, a tall stack of ones
that he fanned out on the kitchen table,
chuckling—his idea of a joke, getting
all this muffled, papery bulk,
when what is really wanted
is a shift in denomination.
Even that young, I could understand
the humor, a smile eking across
my Nordic face, a taste for sorrow.

First Death

My first death needed a little suit, bowtie;
father's mother, never known to me,
was dead downtown, lying in the satin
of her casket. I looked hard for her soul
to move, hard at the hinged lid.

She was never much talked about, but
one story sticks: how she would rush
from house to barn with bowl and spoon,
anxious at the slaughter of a cow
to catch from the neck
the hot, spurting blood
for a fresh blood pudding.

Can I say—knowing only
this?—I see him
bled by her, grayed, dulled,
slumping to his knees
in the steamy immigrant barn.

Still Life with Sisyphus

At rest
in a nest of grass
halfway up Tower Hill,
the boulder begged for boys,
wanted tennis shoes, the crawl
of daring, hands on its cracks
and crags, gauging
its rugged hugeness.
New life on a small globe
we took it solid, complete,
a thing to sit upon, to be.

Early days, ancient,
myself the boulder,
the boulder myself,
I ride the earth like a giant,
a son of giants, gazing down
on the neighborhood, the elmtops,
rooftops, intricate lawns and walks,
across the street the schoolhouse,
the asphalt playground, its fenced
unforgiving hardness.

Unbroken Chain

The sun was always sieved
by a canopy of elms,
soft pearls of time that always
fell randomly to the street,
and darted under our wheels,
as we biked down the corridor
of green—a ride that day,
let's say, to the paved lot
parked half-full of semis,
empty hulks in rows, motionless,
weight on fore-knuckles, waiting
to be hooked up and hauled off,
without a view, no urge for their work.

And we'd sling into their lot,
and circle, and let them be
our witnesses, referees of speed,
of chases, amazing spinouts,
bloody gravel at the knee ignored—
see our pedal-standing triumphs,
bronzed arm up, parading
in the good present tense
like Rameses, like Caesar.

Aunt Inga's Abstract Print

I certainly couldn't see him—
Jesus?—blots, swaths of black
on white. (White on black?) "Oh,"
she'd say, "he's there, like a face
you might pick from the clouds,
or lifting out of leaves. Fill it in,
that's the game."

Like Scrabble, after Sunday dinner,
at her little bungalow on Dupont,
lacework on the queen anne table
and fig-filled cookies on china,
the walnut cuckoo clock clicking
over the game, while her Jesus watched
from somewhere in his frame,
as we struggled with our fates
pulled from the turned-over tiles,
tried to add to the language
already played.

And it was always a quiet room
when she laid down her word,
one by one clicking down her tiles,
the squares that counted most,
always finding a way to reach them,
her thin, translucent hand filling in.

Gethsemane Window

> *What is grace? . . .*
> *To wait in a garden and not call out for a friend.*
> — Deborah Keenan, "Grace"

The dire teenage choices: dressing right,
never being from a family, fighting into a new
age, fighting out of a birth order, rogue feet
trampling havoc around the herd, girl-stupid,
butting heads with absolute ignorance
everywhere.

They give you Jesus at church, another struggling
son. The sanctuary you wander into after choir
is quiet, final purples blooming in the window,
a leaden garden, its cedar, fig, and grape gone black
in a stained-glass dusk. Grief flows milky gray
down his robes, and from somewhere beyond
the panes a radiance is aimed directly at
his face, at the ardor in the angle of that face,
which is not, surely, that a lamplighter
should come to cancel this night,
but that no one has followed this far.

Even his stone bench looks asleep,
in a dream of return to bedrock,
and the hedges no longer edge a path
but have receded back into night.
All but the center of the labyrinth
is subdued, arrested, and the church is dark.

Hwy 61

Out of town, finally on the way,
we sit with our backs to St. Paul,
panning past fenced fields north,
the old green Oldsmobile
like a beetle in the sun
on a straight dash for new cover
along the race of power poles.

North, into the waning of billboards,
and we are stuck on Z, the game dissolving
into a huge unbuilt sky. Blue eyes
out of school, we build new syllables
in the sway of grass, in the slow pattern
of guernseys on a pasture slope—
and that never-expected horse, it bends
its head mythologically to the turf.

I become farsighted, no longer look
for specks of city up ahead. My feet
remember the dark solid granite
spilled along the shore above Duluth—
running the boulders, I am the lake,
I am a glittering aspen leaf.

Revision

Let's start again. This time, I'll
be firstborn, not sixth of eight.
And let's pare the total back
to two, or less. (The leftovers
could turn out to be neighbor
kids.) Then, in the car, everyone
would have a window seat.
Sometimes I'd sit in front, and I'd
chat with Dad. On hot July evenings,
driving back from a placid family
picnic at the lake, in our damp suits
and big soggy towels, we'd stop
at the Dairy Queen and have hot
fudge banana sundaes, large,
not dinky little nickel cones
un-dipped in chocolate.
And I would have my own room,
like on TV. I would sit in my
room with my stuff, and I'd
realize, quite early on, what a
unique individual I am. I
wouldn't need to wait my turn.
It would always be my turn.
Not cast down the well
of birth order, not scrabbling
up dark, slippery stonework, eyes
on the small circle of light above,
I would sit on my bed, pretty much
ok in first draft.

I Knew All Along

Who knew better than me
that hand to mouth these blueberries,
somewhere rocky west of Lutsen,
on a slope above a blue glacial lake,
these were the world's best, and I
was in summer's ripest minute?

Who knew the neighborhood
better than me? Streets, sidewalks,
yards, walls, I crept out from my room,
I jumped fences, I tramped like an ant,
unled, undeterred by the straight stick
or barring finger put across my path.
I knew the grid game all along
but wouldn't play.

Who knew the schoolroom clock
better than me? Time-frozen,
looking out tall wooden windows
that rattled in the winter wind,
a hideous tremor, a note moaned
by powers dark and dreadful
—this I knew.

Everything about snow—
how it fell for me, how it lay
like extra world, an unspent surplus, that I
shoveled into causeways of white, piled not shaped,
all borderless surface sharing itself quietly out
into moonscapes of desolation, polar loneliness,
and the glancing isolation of stars.

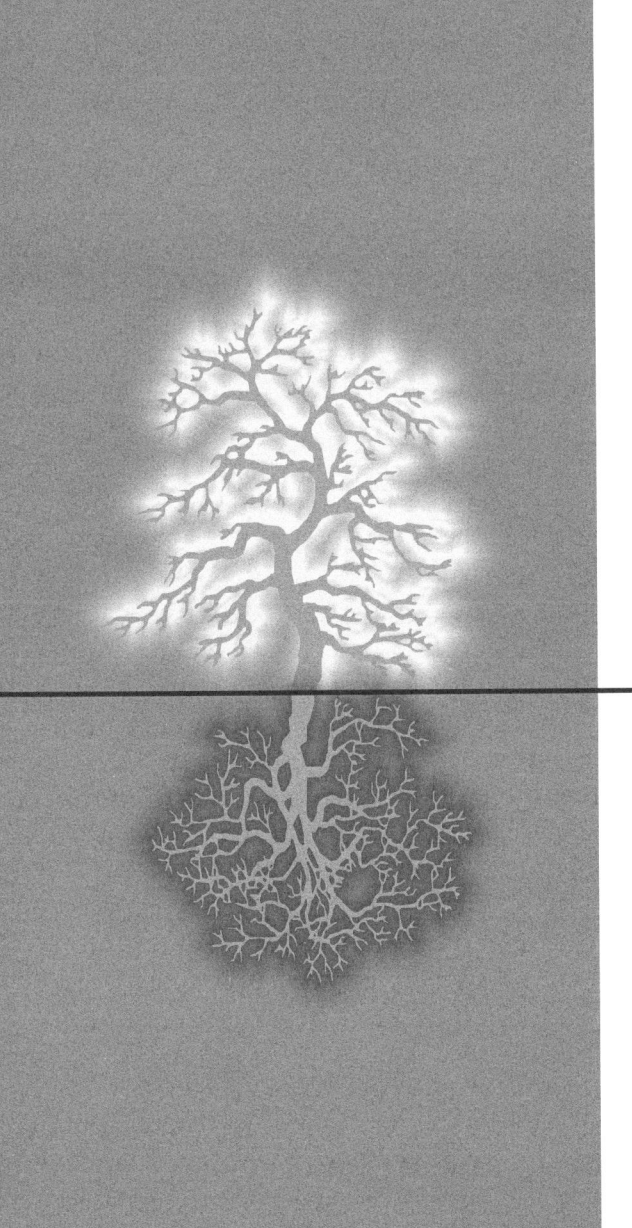

PART TWO

and holding them up to your eye

North Shore Sublunar

She lays down white ribbon
on the blue black lake
and hangs there
holding up her end
as if she knew me
had chosen me
to pilot her slow nightride west.

The front row firs stand ghostly
without eyes in her light
and the wet rocks
their heads deep inside earth
break her shining into shards.
Nothing but the sun ever tells them
what time is—they've never heard
of an age or a night.

It is getting late
and I am still awake
unable for the world to sleep—
still pulling words out of darkness
and holding them up to your eye.

Sundogs Rising

Foetal under blankets,
covered over with house and winter,
I can hear them uncurl from sleep,
pace the muffled room, their claws
clicking on pinewood, settling now
into black breathing heaps
to stare my buried face into birth.

Resisting ascent, I am
dark, heavy-lidded against
another weary round. But stares
keep digging at my will, pull
until—rip warm blankets off, up and
throw the angry curtains apart

upon a total white of new snow
and bright indistinction
flooding sight—
no shift or shade of light,
from yard to field and up the sky
without horizon an equal cloudy white,
all foreground, rounded, close,
untainted by any power
older than the morning.

And I can see I think
a lone hiker out
with two snowbounding dogs,
three gestures in the cold,
brimming up the rise
toward the jagged black front
of that mid-distant grove.

The Face You Almost See

I am the gold scab of lichen
    in among the green,
I am midnight lightning
    printing out an elm,
I am the fit of ancient rock
    against deserted sky,
I am the hollyhock there,
    tall and by itself,
I am the angle of releasing
    under the water's fall,
I am the black half
    of a half moon,
I am the foam
    along a tortured shore,
I am that shape
    on the road up ahead,
I am the red pill
    the robin rips from ivy,
I am gloom
    thick within the copse,
I am what the raccoon clutches
    like a gem,
and the face you almost see
    in a cloud;
I am nothing, nothing at all
    like the sun,
I am a dug up bulb
    shovel split,
I am the depth of a deep hole.

West of Grand Forks

By the road
in early June sun,
in the first few rows
of grass green wheat
each six-inch blade
arches under its sky,
caught by shallow roots
in the grid, as glossy
as teardrop in the wind,
and just as alone, each like a marker
in a vast cemetery.

To look out over the orderly acres
is to see into straw-brown autumn,
into silos topped heavy, dense,
silent behind the yardlight,
after the combines have crawled.

But further out is a rogue strand
of heavy old windbreak cottonwoods
that have strayed down the line
between this field and the next,
a haphazard row of leaning pillars
in search of a sacred precinct.
Brush and birds attend their slow
solitary march, and a gray shower
plowing across the map
drapes down rain
into their mass.

May

Too encouraging, really,
the way the yellow sun
pulls summer up
out of haggard earth—

peonies, already tall, leaning
over waxy leaves, the dutiful ants
grooming their heads;
and robins, standing bibbed

over rising worms, flighty,
they sprint a few feet,
stop, and cock the head
for Persephone; and Hades,

keeper of the full equation,
that easily letting her go.

October

Summer sighs high in the maples,
gusts of un-sustaining wind, exhalations
of fervency, wearying the leaves, just now
going brittle, before their loss of green.

Soon these trees will step from their dresses,
shoulders bare, cooling, and hard as marble,
like weathered Michelangelo torsos,
their muscles still stubborn for structure.

And the first fall of snow, and the next,
will slip through their steady fingers
into the quiet cage of winter
like jewelry into its case,

as they patiently hold their daguerreotype poses,
trusting all the rumors of new clothes.

The Clearing

Genial simplicity of green,
a congregation of grasses
that plashes around the odd rock,
over the unplanned unevenness of ground,
like the infancy of sight;

a muted place, fond of its silence—
though just now a nuthatch
dervishing down a trunk
clicks and whistles at the beetles
roaming beneath the bark—

a silence like stretched canvas
waiting for the brush,
the weight of footfalls
on its soft expanse; and stillness,

as if the rough perimeter
of birches and blueberries
had acted once
in a play about cathedral walls.

Sharpened

The cabbage slice, carved down,
has slumped and fallen over
onto the board, away
from the opened heart,
which holds itself tight, wet,
all its edges sharp, all interior,
still whole.

To Bravery, Late

It is only now,
with the sun climbing up
a last brilliant day, with larch
and maple still acting like May,
and the sting of first frost
standing stiff in the grass, yellow
in the gooseberry patch;

only now that rabbit, unseen
all summer, inches onto the lawn,
fat, cautious, fed on moonlit fields
of solitude, the quietest of friends
in a careful network of fright, her pelt
invisible under fiddlehead ferns,
a blur among the dimes of light
beneath the apple tree,
and nest always near
but easily breached,
the midnight cat fishing in,
and one by one her young ascending
screaming;

only now, so late,
she dares to be seen
nibbling on the final tips of green,
eyes protruding, dark as grapes
abandoned in a bowl.

Subtext

Doves in spring,
whatever they speak,
it goes for beauty.
They keep their balance
nodding yes to ordinary dust,
walk in halts, pivots, struts,
thrill themselves by moving,
tide of silver over quaking skin.

To get aloft, they blast
the air with wingstrokes,
perch on the roofpeak, looking
down, new to the height
and wanting their lover there.

January

In Sears moccasins and flu robe
I pad to the hoarfrost window,
squeeze a blot of glass clear
with the hot ham of my thumb
and bend to the cold watery hole.

Out in the bare lilacs
a convocation of sparrows
hunches, fluffs, bows
into the last of the sun,
their pipes of breath
snapped away in ten-below
gusts. In weak dollops
of day's-end light they ride
the black twigs, chattering
invincible infants.

Alarmed
for their feet
and the harder cold tonight,
I hug myself, my gray flesh,
and glance to the schoolyard tree
where the meagre sun is
held in its stiff web of dormant limbs.

Antiphonal

There's no rubric to tell me what I mean
calling to the cardinal in the mulberry tree.

The only bird that answers, he can't decide
what my whistling wants, keeps piping

back, plucky for clues, bending over
his pulpit, peering down. Back

and forth, mimicking timbre and tone,
what he begins I can't add to, practically

autistic in my plastic lawn chair—
Hey There! Hey There (What)! Hey There!

Hey There (What)!—the What hanging,
mute grace note in the rafters of the yard.

IPHIGENEIA

She's right out there in the front yard,
under the peonies, buried early
in spring, a beauty of a calico cat, old,
wrapped in a thin, marine blue kimono
and a homespun Guatemalan shawl.

Iphi, Iphi! If you called her, eventually
she'd show up, braid herself around
your pant leg, your hang-down arm,
writhe in the grass, lovely, dangerous,
take your hand with uninstructed ecstasy.

And how many litters—four, five?—
mated with whom?—kittens scraped
from every part of the palette,
long-hairs, shorts, tabbies, calicoes,
tiny to big, rusty, gray, walnuts to whites—

out of vanity, for the variety, we said,
like a Swede giving birth to Chinese,
a carp to seahorses, a swan to desire;
and we named them all, as they waddled
to the nipple and away to the world—

Darla, Dharma Boy, Ginger, Carl. But,
depleted by the labors in the end,
last litter, she dropped limp little parcels
in odd corners of the house—done
with motherhood. And gone so thin,

bony back and clumpy fur; the hard jump
to the couch, and food, so little; sleep, sleep;
and down to the basement, a purrless
rattle, the last grave night—Iphi, Iphi!
midwife to peonies, spring after spring.

Hound of Earth

We named you Freyja,
that hard-hammered goddess,
Norse wife, stubborn under Thor;
and you, as strong as glacier under leash,
tether taut as gallows rope; no, not to heel
stride ever, without a shout, or whack,
burly flanks churning after scent—
through grasses, bush, mud, snow,
the icy spoor and every rotted ort,
you loved your earth more than men.

Still there, I often think, and almost feel
your bounding planet around my walking,
plowing and playing your substance—
I, in space merely, a carried head
body-tall off the ground, still needing
your low nose out to the trail

spanning me back to home.

America

A man digs in the weeds behind his garage.
Eight or nine generations ago
his blood-mother carried a child
out of a hut
out of a forest, west
toward Norse waters.

In his garden cart
he has eight or nine
bristling rolls of sod
to cover his last plot
of unturned prairie
beside the alley asphalt.

He doesn't notice the fireweed
or the twinleaf
or the milkweed,
the last for eight or nine miles around,
that in his wilting heap
now lie dying.

August

North at night the road gropes
out beyond the weave, an old rope
pulling me out into summer dark,
my headlights reel in scrub like sparks,
flare out wide through the curves,
blinding the trees, leaving everything disturbed;
then straightening past a low-slung knoll,
I freeze the leap of a crossing doe.

Slam down brakes, heave
to a halt—blocked, in night's cave,
where life to life we're chained,
worlds edge to edge, crickets
ringing, and great Lascaux eyes
flashing back all my harsh light.

And slow, slow as the zodiac,
her tall foreleg lifts; and back
through a parting of brush,
the flag of her tail tall, vanished—
an old blade pulled from an old wound.

Narrative

The image is still there
from last winter, of driving
in the bleached aftermath
of a harsh prairie blizzard,
when I sped down under an underpass
on a still-unplowed highway, fast,
or so it seemed with all the wind,
wind by which a pigeon living there
was taken in its sudden thought to fly
and thrown like mud at my windshield,
thudded dead-on like a movie
into my real car, and was shrugged off
tumbling like a man overboard
into the wake of snow beside the road.

Looking back, craning back,
rearview mirror—and nothing rose
slate and cream and living
from the blown white roadside;
and I shrank into livid grief
for the scores and scores
of centuries that have driven,
drive us now, in the vanguard
of their churn, leashed beasts
storming through Eden.

And I kept going,
exactly like time,
easily abstract, home.

Frodo in the Yard

Head and shoulders above the bracken,
he stands under the centuries-old oak,
modeled in red clay, hooded head, squatty body,
forever slipping on the ring—or slipping it off,
it cannot be said which.

But there he is, like a toggle switch
between dream and this hazy green day,
gazing down at his ceramic finger,
caught between worlds, transfixed,
permanently hardened into this one.

He cannot be said to notice
the black clouds, just now prowling
over the hill, that send before them
a chill wind sluicing through the screen porch
and out across the stormy bend-over grass;

or the harder gust, just now leaning
into heavy limbs over the roof,
setting a sea of leaves screaming,
so that oak twigs drop around the porch,
let go alive into the pitching yard.

One, clumsy with leaves, thuds
onto the walk like a pushed refugee
gripping luggage in the windswept open.
Further blows kick it up the flagstones,

as it scrapes along resisting,
twists toward the screen door,
and stumbles up against the bottom grille,
where it is held for a moment,
pressed at mid-death,
unsure what passage this is.

Last Year's Web

A fat July fly, she got in somehow.
I watch her scud screen to screen
shopping the porch in her best metallic
green. Barrier by barrier, she blimps
vaguely into a corner, where a black
filthy web is slung in its last year's haunt,
spiderless now—but still she gets caught
in this bit of history, and tries to crawl away
dragging it, tugs but cannot free her feet,
repeats and repeats—but it's no use.

I put my finger on her buzzing body, swipe
at the old, weightless web; and it feels
like something saving me
as she flies free.

PART THREE

*leaning into
something
unseen*

Imago Patris

To think I am the result
of his steaming home from Belgium,
of Army garb gladly cast off, epaulets,
harsh woolens, sinking to the floor,
in a room, in a warm October bed,
egg and the final seeking lunge
for reunion. O harbor song
of the smallest craft
plying the breast of the sea,
back from Normandy,
I—the result?—voyeur now of my launch,
gone squeamish, almost blushing
at my loss of privacy, eyeglass trained
across time.

And now he is gone,
faded to ash, as I too fade
behind him, a three decades' march,
three and a half, the same gray-blue eyes
picking the hardest ways home,
my feet placed precisely, heavily,
hauling the furniture, his limp outmoded clothes,
his hammers and clamps, a lifetime
of brads in a box—up from the basement,
a last walk down the halls of the house,
never to be emptied of his passage,
in the wake of his taking leave.

A Road

through the permanent dusk of an old French rubber plantation,
thrown from the Jeep, crashing down through senseless limbs
to the ground, lacerated everywhere, unconscious, hip broken,
trucked in the dark to base camp, semi-conscious, lashed
to an outboard stretcher, a helicopter to Bien Hoa MASH Unit,
days, nights, and the good helicopter to Saigon, French stuccoed
pavilion, strapped in bed in arch-softened light, finally a flight up
over the Pacific, howling pitching thunderstorm, ditch, ditch to
Japan, ambulance, unnamed airbase to unnamed city hospital,
oriental eyes calm over the bed, back up over water next day,
Oakland, stainless steel, linen, buzz of American care, a prop
to Denver, sprawling Army hospital, guy in the next bed no legs.

A free phone call home from the bed: "Yes, Denver! Yes!"

The Chevy loaded, waxed, he backs it up the new asphalt
driveway, where she stands at the top with her purse, ready,
and down the elm-dappled street, crosstown, out of town,
cornfields, alfalfa, formica coffee shops, Holiday Inns,
Triple-A StripMap down Minnesota, dipping into Iowa,
west over endless Nebraska, and up onto the high plains,
watching the Rocky tops rise into Colorado air—closing
with the boy, him alone, sitting up on the edge of his bed,
first time in strapped-down weeks, fragile, giddy; and a breeze
through the open window, it blows him over
into their arms. It blows him over.

Dad's Lamps (Two Beauties)

When quiet in the evening
one of them stuns my eye
and I am brought back
to his basement workshop,
I put down my book:

low-ceilinged clutter, the shavings
under the lathe of his retirement,
where he stood with his gouge
laid against chattering wood, trying again
for the perfect sweep of elimination.

Cartons of blocky knickknacks
came up the basement stairs, sold
to little shops, given away,
birthdays, Christmases, gone
to family, friends—me.

It was seldom
he felt the gods of beauty
in his own thick hands—
hands with bitter farm, war
and too little school in them,
too many businesslike handshakes.

And retiring early did not help
to write the novel. No story
in him—none he could find—
he stood at his second-best post,
searching the turning wood
for what lay hidden there.

All the Usual Cars

All the usual cars are parked out front, who's there,
who's not there yet, clear. She's had to endure so
many of these, but puts up with it better than me.
I make sure I'm lagging a little with the presents so
she's first in the door, good at greeting, the show.
After tipping them under the tree, all I know is
I want a cigarette and solitude, for it to be gotten through
and home again, talking out all the usual irks and nuances.
Her family is as weird as mine, but talky, voluble,
and smaller, with the public faces preachers' kids learn
by now delved, exposed, vestigial. I have them to look forward to
tomorrow. For now, I press a rather sullen face through
the evening, once again amazed at how fluently she gets on
with my family. We want none of this, really, craving release
from the cycle of holidays, gatherings, our part of the meal
assigned, brought in a traveling dish, we bringing no
new generation to the table, but hungering for some other
reunion around an as yet unfound fireside, somewhere
by water, in our own winter, remote, wholly rustic,
only an impassable road leading to the door.
There, a table, a window, and without distraction
the images of being could be fastened to a page. She'd
be free to write, her powers, as she says, no longer
under a cloud. But I buy lottery tickets against the future,
as my Dad did, even at eighty-five. And I settle again
into reading the Greek from Luke, she
the Portuguese, and so on around the room,
language by language, verse by verse, again.

Appointment

They say, when parents die,
suddenly nothing stands
between you and your death—
queued to the front, you
are the next to dive,
and reality is your toes
gripping the edge
of the board, feeling
the roughened surface,
sensitive feet, softened
by years in the shallows.

Your calamity is your lack
of practice, resisting the nudges
you've had, like Apollo on Olympus,
always shooting your arrows from safety.
Now you are struck, you
are leaning into the pike.

But only one did die—two
gaping years ago—and between
appointments, you do no more
than tarry, out of the pool,
needing, not needing, a towel,
fumbling with phrases, the metrics
of middle age, and Mother so old,
knowing the Sibylline schedule,
and the air getting cold.

The Home

Elevator to the seventh floor.
She is in. They are all in,
behind their doors, lucky
to be still in this wing.

Museum of last kept things,
door after door, we might enter
each diorama—after a soft knock,
the slow trudge to a living room.

She seats me on her new couch,
her sign that life is continuing,
but it is still like traveling light
and getting nowhere.

So many small remembrances—
odd to sit amongst—the house
they were brought from gone, the
husband, the garden for that vase.

STROKE

She winces mid-sentence,
knows the next noun is lost
in a darkened pond of words,
and glares at me, embarrassed.

About Eleanor, Mother,
you were telling me
how she isn't really a friend,
talks and talks, visits
without warning, leaves no room
for you—and she kisses you,
on the lips, when she leaves?

Yes, she kisses me! Can you...
believe it? I don't know her that...
sagging back
into her pillow,
mumbling mildly,
all the right side of her body
gone.

The ward. Tiled final hallways,
door after door, a curtained, uncurtained,
crèche...
I bend over the failure of flesh,
to make it good with a kiss, like this,
years, surely, since the last;
she who showed me kiss from kiss,
stroke the drowsing cheek,
and lightly, a seraph over the temple,
letting go with a wisp of hair
through fingertips.

The Founding Fathers

There they are in their photographs, grandfathers,
great-grandfathers (and mothers, seated), proof
of the new land, a strong arm, looking travel weary
in their sepia duds, all the way from Oslo,
standing before a painted studio backcloth
in hard farmer poses.

Round-eyed, they look straight at us like crops
or cattle, not so sure this new lens understands
the providence, or how they want to soften it forward.
We pass the antique images around the dining room table,
with humor, or silence, but not much wonderment.
We are there to divide them up. To take them home
for the next dividing.

First Marriage: Syntax

We didn't need adjectives
in the dark, didn't fumble
for the bon mot. Like the first phrase
in a long, confident sentence,
we made a good start.

Subjects of our objects,
in the griefless joinery
of being each other's
noun, nuance, self,
and with perfect timing—
these didn't seem fragments,
but they were never enough.

Way down the page now,
and I am a relative clause
letting myself down a rope
of remembrance, hanging
again in that clouded speech,

> *But, do you—do you really?*
> *Of course. Of course I do.*
> *It's the dinner, then.*
> *Yes, the dinner—the season, the year. A starless sky.*

predicates in a mist,
we are homonyms apart,
grabbing for something meant.

Wordplay; *that* you cannot play at
without having already flung yourself
into another sentence, to nurse
infinitives that *were* split.

Who Knew

for Sylvia

I'm sure the park bench knew,
feeling our heat
on cool evening planks;
and the darkening bushes too,

I'm sure they knew,
joining hands in their secret way,
feeling quite protective, in fact,
now they had a job to do;

and the grass knew everything,
as the wise dusk crept in
to cup the flame
without a word.

July

A thin strip of sun
has been dialing across the carpet
all morning. And now
it has swept past noon
and has me cornered on the couch,
where, in perfect physics, it climbs
my shoulder, bleeds down my arm,
paints the back of my hand with light.

I see the lit up years, baked in,
lizard toughness permanent, texture
etched hard into age that can't come back.
Prod the specimen, test it, spread
the skin smooth: it springs back
to the correct time. Raise fingers to
a pose of grip: they stand like trees
leaning into something unseen.

Eyesore

Get out pruning shears, bow saw, shovel;
spring has not revived the roots or leaves
of the cherry bush—that skeleton there
by the front walk, a scar on the hedgerow.

I dismantle it branch by branch, sad
as I go, cut, pull it from the stubborn
grip of its hedge mates, strip away the twigs,
make piles of its complicated life.

A quick job and then done, I'm thinking,
as I bend for a first bundle—which shifts
as I gather it, and one blunt branch-end
swings hard into my unshut eye; and with

an instantaneous knowledge of hurt
I stop, stand, stare out, test my gashed vision,
a liquid, curtaining world flowing in,
branches in my hand swimming in the wound.

How We've Done It for—Years

for Paul

Starting small over coffee,
the usual tabletop, ashtray,
hands in place, words delivered
with fixity of eyes, tipping
this king against that deuce,
a house of cards rising,
an ace passed like a wafer
over an altar, balancing
on the lip of the other,
tent of talk that trembles
when an ash is knocked
or a hand moves uncharmed—
building the edifice up,
two one-eyed jacks
standing on the top tier
carrying a queen
over their heads.

NOVEMBER

This morning,
a new skin of ice on the river
smothers the slower flow near shore
and lets the middle meander through.
Low rags of fog blur a barge
floating in its warm belief
in a homecoming, *New Orleans*
on its hull.

From high above, where I stand
at the rail on Lake Street bridge,
the clogged gorge looks pensive,
almost willing to pause
in this town, to eddy in place
translating the sky's trouble
into inwardness, and be taken
by ice, and rest, past midpoint
in the loss of light, heat,
the crystalline sheet growing,
closing from either shore.

My Life, So Far

Truly, I don't remember standing there in pajamas,
holster and sixguns strapped on, stunned blots

of kodak light staring from the Christmas tree
that fills in the background with spiky complexity.

Jimmy was always three years and three days older,
and he's got his new pistol drawn, convincingly

pointing it at the camera—quite the little desperado.
I don't remember a pose like this from him, ever;

but then, I was always mainly catching up—even
there, I see, I'm looking down at my holstered gun

as at some horrendous growth clinging to my hip.
My weapons were never shiny like this, never so heavy:

swift, light, hidden, I think of grace, as in
a smooth communion with a ball, as in quietly

lifting the cookie jar lid, reaching down deep
for my own private portion, always stealing more.

Then dawn, and it's my watch, guarding the Viet Cong Colonel
who sits peacefully in his makeshift barbed-wire cage.

No name, I don't remember his face; I
remember his age-old glance,

as he gives a little tipping sign for wanting water,
and I come in to him with my olive drab canteen.

Much later, and I'm glad I left my rifle there—did not re-
member leaning it, near his hand, to pour his bowl full

of dark drink—though he never took it up. Word was,
they flung him, next day, high from an olive drab chopper;

and time after time, I fall from the sky, swift and light, looking
for a landing, somewhere hidden, and green enough, and new.

Experience

—is it like chard then?
A large harvest, and it keeps growing,
shoulder over shoulder; but bring in armfuls
and it boils down to a blot on your plate.

And please,
pass the Swedish meatballs
—yes, potatoes too.

I look past my Minneapolis meal
into Europe, Asia, the ancient feasts:
give me a Delphic spring
to feed my Minnehaha Falls,
give me mysteries and orioles
diving through my mind,
clean as oranges, clearly prayer.

Like Hiawatha, like medicine,
scout out the old words,
track them out of Athens, out of Ur.

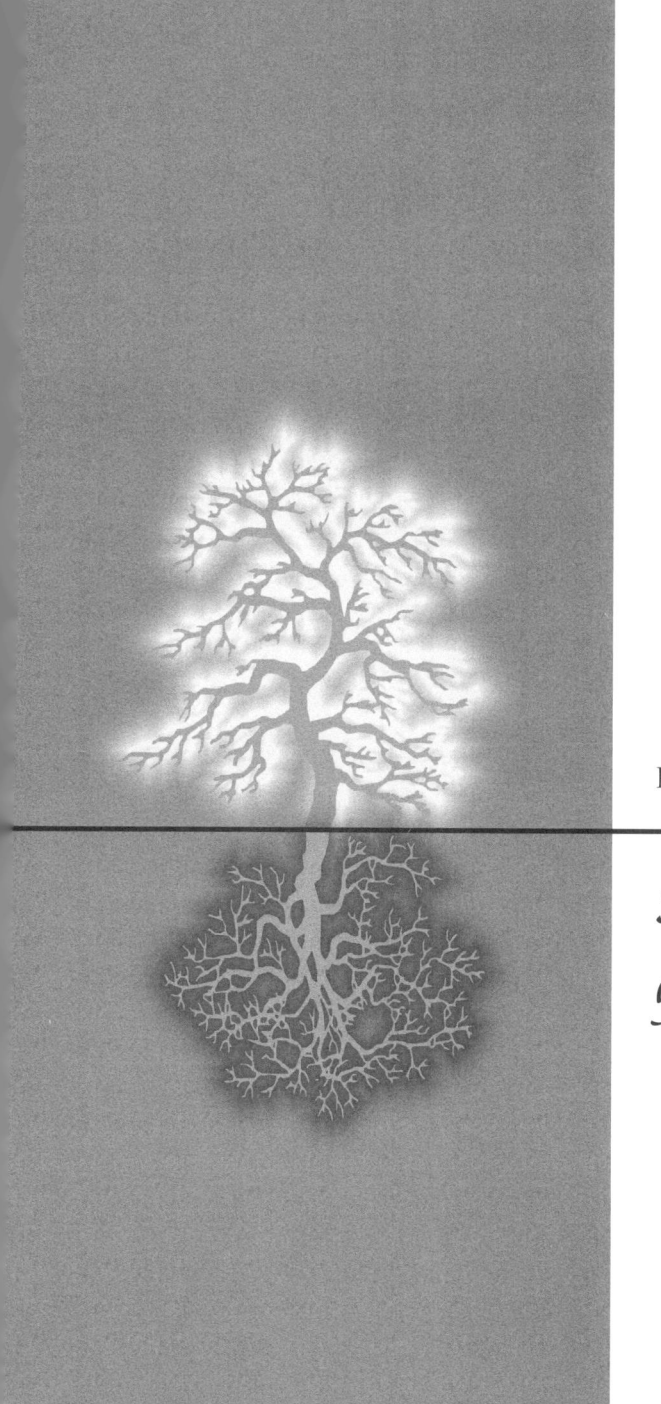

PART FOUR

Shall we go down?

A Gnostic Gospel

In the middle of nowhere
with an armload of light
I always pick the closest shadow
to pry at like a scab.

I am Archimedes in the street
popping manhole covers—
they flip up and wobble away
leaving the shafts exposed.

See, there are footholds.
Shall we go down?

All Hallows' Eve

The lengthening shadow of the spent day
sips the last thin light from every pool;
only fools, sleepers through the change, smile away.

No treats, no tarot tricks or sandbox play,
no weeping huggers or mother tuggers, will fool
the lengthening shadow of the spent day.

Demons, unannounced, visit holy trays
of body, blood, and pigeon. Chaos rules;
only fools, sleepers through the change, smile away.

Menorah candles cannot light the way
bright enough to thwart the claw, the drool,
the lengthening shadow of the spent day.

Spindly bridges, arched above the disarray,
have no footing, no piers set with jewels;
only fools, sleepers through the change, smile away.

Some seer may have spoken, may yet say
where to kneel, where to find renewal,
while the lengthening shadow of the spent day
only fools sleepers through the change, miles away.

Jeremiad

Absolutely
disregard the snarling guards;
the old rooms are empty,
and faces out on the perimeter
are watching the hard slippage
having already counted the loss.

Deep shattering chords
are not as low or loud
as they can go, not
while still the wrench and shift
stun waiting hearts
with peals across the night.

Bloodshot whites
of a billion eyes brace
against the blind side
that twines with turmoil
and beetles over crouching heads
like lava over towns.

The well
of the mounting past
is not dry
or stopped
by any Eden
in time.

sonnet nine one one oh one

they want you to tell them how you feel
how you felt when you heard
when you saw no when you took
that crushing fuselage through your chest

how did it feel being born
thrust out of your mother's body
onto clean white receiving sheets
a mess of blood and bewilderment

yes and no memory for it now
no inner album no fleshy glossies
no gasps or slaps to launch you
on a lyric of how it felt feels was

to see those cathedral doors open
purple of the goddess in your veins

Before Pilate

I was a spike not far from original ore.
I was heavy in the tongs that lifted me from the fire.
I was slendered and pointed for the work.
I was blunted one end for the blows.
I was made ready for the hammer.
I was pounded through flesh into olive.

I am harder than what I pass through.
I feel the wood stubborn for form.
I feel a weight heavy on my back.
I cannot see beyond this sentence.

Garden Mary

Often-repeated stone and gaudy
paint, she stands grottoed
in an unkempt corner of lilac,
of lilies brawling with peonies.
She seems not to have been
waiting for me, or for this
spring green day. Sequestered
in leeward calm, years and seasons
out of mind, the sculptor gone
and the shrinemaker, her face
bends on some private, infinite
nearness.   I hesitate
with my rake. Shall I scrape
a wet year of leaves from her bed,
come pawing at the column
of her skirts like a vandal?
And if I do, won't the beetles
and grubs trundle and worm,
follow her ripening dark
to the hidden face of the moon?
But she will not move, wanting
only perhaps the rising loam,
the body touch of earth,
and to sink in the slow loosening of stone.

Joan in the Wood

She had seen to the setting of logs,
had stacked them handsomely, the fuel
which that other fuel, thin air,
would join; and come the heat, the flame,
nothing mild or tentative would stop
the union, the wild dance into spirit.

Cabin cold, night falling—what spirit,
she wondered, living deep in these logs,
wants merely to be burnt up, not stop
until brought to nothing, the fuel
for a brilliance, for a brief hot flame,
then cabin cold again, the freezing air.

And, she thought, that other fuel, the air,
is it waiting there, like the wood, to spirit
itself into a difference; or does it flame
around its lover, this dull stack of logs,
to no purpose more than surge, a fuel,
that once consumed will merely stop?

Cabin cold, dawn far off—and what can stop
this thought that night weighs most? Black air
stares in the window, bodiless, blank, a fuel
for dead thoughts, for loss of heart, spirit,
which seems now to settle in the room, on the logs,
in the hearth—no spark for any flame.

Again, she has a match. But she has often seen a flame,
and smoke, and waves of heat, which did not stop
till nothing but an ashen heap remained of logs;
then grate grew cold, and cold took the air—
over and over, in her diary, page after page, spirit
snuffed. She went to these pages as if for fuel.

Cabin cold, hour of silent wings—new fuel
is ready, and she is ready for the flame.
She closes the sour book, lets its teary spirit
shrink away from world. Stop, she says, stop
gazing in a mirror. Run fingers through the air,
help it hold a bigger thing than me, than logs.

For the spirit, she is fuel.
She strikes a flame, she does not stop
—heavy air moves in around the logs.

Elvis

His brow is rising, eyes
out of Egypt, frightening,
like a storm come alive,
lightning, his hips seething
Mississippi riverbanks,
waist down in Memphis,
a mud of sweat and leather,
a man-boy face too smooth, the mouth
as tragic as anything Athenian;

Parian marble, wrenched
from the plinth grinning,
he bends over an ode
and breaks as he moves,
as the Greek chorus croons
good-ol'-boy gospel, Tennessee tunes,
plainly insane to be that close up,
seeing the mystery, the other side
of everything flashing on the waters.

She Told Me the Story of Her Life

Athelas said: Just now, I'm free. Totally. Gotta put your name in the book here though. Then I'll be right over. The bookbag can go with you, over there, by my wastebasket. Name?

Well, so what's it going to be? Like this? and just over the ear, like so? like, here? Up with the bangs a little? —the front, I mean. I do so many women, too. Comfortable with either. Not much different, really. Y' know? Hair's hair.

Only, no, it's not "Othella." It's "Athelas."

Yes, I suppose it is "very unusual." Really. But, I mean, nobody else. Ever. Schools I started, all the same with starting out weird—"What's the name?" —y'know?

This is just water. It gets the length of things clear, exposed. Wow, getting thin up here. Hardly feel it in the comb. I lean, you know, so if you don't like the touching, just keep the elbows in. It's not like I'm—you know. Just relaxed. Tired, sort of. Everybody else gets to sit.

But, yeah, it was my mom with the name thing. Hippie mom, beads, tie-dye. Tolkien, she said, a plant in Tolkien. She was reading a lot of it pregnant. I guess it's some sort of plant in Tolkien.

Judy or something, or Katy—ha!—that would've been dumb, too. Like a really boring tattoo. Block the back, Sir, shortish? or buzz from nothing, clippers?

Nope. No dad to say how dumb it was.

Never did look it up. —Magical elven healing powers? Really? Is the beard o.k. today, Sir? Good. I usually goof 'em up. Guys learn not to trust me with their faces.

Close your eyes. Yes. Good. (I love the closing eyes.) There. Done. It's all over.

At Orchestra Hall

Almost comfortable in my seat, in my certain captured niche, those things, that is, one knows, which are, of course, the best sorts of things, one's private history of the godforsaken world, like a movie of sorts, ongoing, always being revised, the psyche having to put up with a lot, new things seldom being better things, just additional fuel for dismay; like Boccherini, having just now been rendered as if he were Mozart, tinklingly shallow, or like that radiant woman there, across the plush lobby carpet, statuesque, dramatically at ease, yet so remote from any possible outcome; and I, who stand by my fluted pillar, instinctively gathering a narrative of approach, a welling up of passion closing on some half-hidden remark that will charm and fugue us both, will transport our private cosmos to its next chord, a blythe incorporation that, as I stir my intermission drink, swizzle stick oaring through the ice, glides like a longboat into a steep and lonely fjord.

Aubade

It is always later, after the transaction,
that I count my change. Did you mean
you loved me—or were we dancing
marionettes, clacking out lines
for the sake of the stage,
swung on our strings
into a way of seeming?
I couldn't reach for you,
the strings held me back,
and my set poses
wouldn't bend.

In my traveling case,
here in the dark, I rue
the cruel strings, and I rue the stage
where I can't grasp a thing.
Was your face set that way
at the factory, or were you
really that pleased?
I'm ready now.

Then

Before, I had nothing to say. Then I did.
The front porch door never did close
properly, easily. Something to do with
the set of the hinges, the way the stiles
of the door always wanted to warp
against them. I fixed it twice. Then,
a new door. A carpenter this time.
But it was still the same. After a bit.

So, I was glad it wasn't just me. But
it's still hard going out and coming in.
Always the wrestling, into the world,
out of it, and the warping south sun
dazzling in your face, or daggers
on your returning back.

Caesura

Sometimes you reach an end of seeing,
where every angle of light seems to have fallen
just so before. Not if, but when have these trees
held out their limbs so willfully before, and
into such familiar air? Earth's weight,
each color, stand spellbound—a moment
so clear, that not even the squirrel
circling the birdbath for seeds
can dig commas in what is finished here.

And when the towering sky begins to move,
you, too, are left to circle again alone.

TOM RUUD lives in St. Paul, Minnesota, with his wife, Sylvia, and two dogs, Sparky and Pepper. He holds a BA Degree in Classics from Augsburg College, and an MFA Degree in Writing from Hamline University. He is recipient of a Lake Superior Writers Competition Award, a Loft Mentor Series Fellowship, and a Minnesota State Arts Board Fellowship. He teaches at The Loft Literary Center in Minneapolis, and privately.

LAUREL
POETRY
COLLECTIVE

A gathering of twenty-three poets and graphic artists living in the Twin Cities area, the Laurel Poetry Collective is a collaboration dedicated to publishing beautiful and affordable books, chapbooks, and broadsides. Started in 2002, its four-year charter is to publish and celebrate, one by one, a book or chapbook by each of its twenty-one poet members. The Laurel members are: Lisa Ann Berg, Teresa Boyer, Annie Breitenbucher, Margot Fortunato Galt, Georgia A. Greeley, Ann Iverson, Mary L. Junge, Deborah Keenan, Joyce Kennedy, Ilze Kļaviņa Mueller, Yvette Nelson, Eileen O'Toole, Kathy Alma Peterson, Regula Russelle, Sylvia Ruud, Tom Ruud, Su Smallen, Susanna Styve, Suzanne Swanson, Nancy M. Walden, Lois Welshons, Pam Wynn, Nolan Zavoral.

For current information about the series—including broadsides, subscriptions, and single copy purchase—visit:

www.laurelpoetry.com

or write:

Laurel Poetry Collective
1168 Laurel Avenue
St. Paul, MN 55104

NORMANDALE COMMUNITY COLLEGE
LIBRARY
9700 FRANCE AVENUE SOUTH
BLOOMINGTON, MN 55431-4399